More Praise for *Stop Struggling with Your Teen*

"A parents' 'survival guide' to dealing with teens. . . . A handy, no-nonsense Baedeker. *Stop Struggling with Your Teen* addresses problems ranging from truancy, drugs, and sex to overloud stereos."

—*Family Circle*

"In less than an hour, you can learn how to get along with your eight- to eighteen-year-old."

—*Saint Louis Post-Dispatch*

"We confidently recommend that all parents read it *before* their children get into their teens. It can sensitize parents to the potential behavioral storm that adolescence can bring into a family."

—Richard Johnson, Ph.D.,
Saint Louis Academy of Family Physicians Newsletter

PENGUIN BOOKS
STOP STRUGGLING WITH YOUR TEEN

Evonne Weinhaus and Karen Friedman have been featured guests on "The Today Show," "Hour Magazine," and "The Sally Jessy Raphael Show." They have also been featured in *Family Circle*, *McCall's*, and *Woman's Day* magazines, as well as major city newspapers across the country.

EVONNE WEINHAUS is a nationally licensed counselor with master's degrees in counseling, psychology, and education. She earned her B.A. at Washington University, M.A.T. at Webster University, and M.A. in Counseling Psychology from the Alfred Adler Institute in Chicago. A family and marriage counselor affiliated with Comprehensive Clinical Consulting Services, she also provides consultation and training to schools, colleges, and professional organizations, and gives workshops nationwide. She lives in Saint Louis with her husband, Sheldon, and their three teenagers.

KAREN FRIEDMAN is a nationally certified clinical social worker. She earned her B.A. at Hunter College and her M.S.W. at the University of Missouri at Saint Louis; she has four years' postgraduate work at the Alfred Adler Institute in Chicago. She has held adjunct faculty positions at the Saint Louis University School of Medicine, Webster University, and Jane Adams School of Social Work. Currently, she provides clinical and consulting services to clients in Saint Louis, where she resides with her husband, Chuck, and their three children.

Stop Struggling

with Your Teen

Evonne Weinhaus
and Karen Friedman

Illustrations by
Marian M. Amies

PENGUIN BOOKS

PENGUIN BOOKS
Published by the Penguin Group
Viking Penguin Inc., 40 West 23rd Street,
New York, New York, 10010, U.S.A.
Penguin Books Ltd, 27 Wrights Lane,
London W8 5TZ, England
Penguin Books Australia Ltd, Ringwood,
Victoria, Australia
Penguin Books Canada Ltd, 2801 John Street,
Markham, Ontario, Canada L3R 1B4
Penguin Books (N.Z.) Ltd, 182–190 Wairau Road,
Auckland 10, New Zealand

Penguin Books Ltd, Registered Offices:
Harmondsworth, Middlesex, England

First published in the United States of America by
J. B. Speck Press 1984
This expanded edition published in Penguin Books 1988
Published simultaneously in Canada

LIBRARY OF CONGRESS CATALOGING IN PUBLICATION DATA
Weinhaus, Evonne.
Stop struggling with your teen.
1. Youth—United States—Family relationships.
2. Child rearing—United States.   3. Adolescence
psychology.   I. Friedman, Karen, 1951–   .   II. Title.
HQ796.W369   1988   649'.125   87-7152
ISBN 0 14 010604 9

Printed in the United States of America by
R. R. Donnelley & Sons Company, Harrisonburg, Virginia
Set in Century Expanded
Designed by Victoria Hartman
Illustrations by Marian M. Amies

Dedication

This manual is based on the work of Robert Bayard, Ph.D., and Jean Bayard, Ph.D., authors of *How to Deal with Your Acting-Up Teenager*. Working with Bob helped us find an approach to parenting that blends a calm, caring attitude with a determination to protect parental rights. Bob and Jean have touched the lives of many grateful parents and teens, and they have touched our lives as well. We want to thank them both for their inspiration.

Acknowledgments

We would like to thank Karen Kotner for her insight and direction, Shel Weinhaus for his undaunting encouragement, Chuck Friedman for his lack of negativism, Mary Kummer's peer-counseling class at Parkway Central High School for contributing the teen's point of view, Mary Williams, our typist, for her patience, and, of course, our clients.

Acknowledgements

Foreword

Many books describe the plight of the parent-adolescent relationship; few, however, provide as clear a step-by-step means for effectively changing it as *Stop Struggling with Your Teen*. Evonne and Karen's manual outlines clear, concise, practical instructions on how to communicate with a teen without fighting.

I recommend this book to *all* parents. Those now struggling with teens can benefit immediately. Parents of younger children can get a head start on utilizing the techniques and concepts that promote a positive parent-child relationship. As a parent and therapist, I can assure you this book will help.

Laura Herring, M.A., Ed.
Marriage and Family Therapist

Contents

I

Changing Your Attitude

1

Changing Your Attitude

In the Beginning

The parent-teen relationship is unpredictable—so unpredictable it can turn your whole family upside down. You may find it comforting to know that most teenagers come out of the adolescent period right-side up. But in the meantime, many parents find themselves in a confusing and frustrating position. They have tried everything to create a healthy and harmonious atmosphere, but, for reasons they can't understand, they end up living in turmoil. Both adults and adolescents are left feeling discouraged and defeated.

3

As a parent, you may have tried some of the following methods of discipline:

Grounding: "You stayed out past curfew again. Now you're grounded for the week."

Rewards: "I'll give you fifteen dollars for every 'A' you get."

Guidance: "If you don't do your homework, you'll flunk out. Then you won't be able to get a good-paying job."

Supervision: "I am going to take you to and from school every day and check with your teachers once a week."

Understanding: "Why do you do these things? Let's talk about it so I can understand what's going on."

Orders: "Take the garbage out now."

Pleading: "I don't ask that much from you. Please take your dirty dishes out of the den."

If you've found that some of these approaches work well with your teenager, stick with them! Don't tamper with success! However, if these methods aren't working and you are at your wit's end, it may be time to take a look at what's going on.

More than likely you have been doing one or both of the following:

1. Trying to run your teenager's life.
2. Failing to make your own life happy.

In this manual, we will give you a plan to turn this situation around. We would like you to take each step seriously and spend some time on it. You might want to browse through the manual first to get an idea of the total picture, but then we recommend sitting down and working through the entire process as it is presented. It seems reasonable that you should see some changes within six to eight weeks. As you continue to incorporate the ideas presented in this manual, not only will you see improvement, but in addition, both you and your teenager will gain a sense of self-satisfaction. You deserve the chance to be calm and happy, and your teenager deserves the chance to learn that he can be self-sufficient and run his own life.

Binding Your Happiness to Your Teen's Behavior

We will begin by taking a look at how you may have stopped taking care of yourself, because, before changing your relationship with your teen, you have to help yourself feel better. **All too often parental feelings of happiness are replaced with guilt, worry, and frustration. When this happens, parents develop an attitude that *binds* their happiness to the teenager's behavior.**

Some common parental attitudes that can tie you to your teenager in this way are:

1. I'm always here to serve.
2. He's too young to use sound judgment.
3. What will other people think?
4. My kid is like a ball of clay that has to be molded.

These attitudes assume that you are entirely in charge of your child's actions, and that the teen is not capable of being responsible. When you see things this way, you put your own thoughts, feelings, and wishes aside, and respond only to what your teen needs. Ultimately, you can end up sacrificing your own serenity and happiness.

Here's an example of what we are talking about:

Let's say your teenager makes a habit of arriving late for dinner because he has been out cruising with "undesirable" friends. You dutifully serve his dinner when he arrives home late as you complain about *his* tardiness and *his* choice of friends.

Parent: "Where were you?"

Teen: No answer.

Parent: "Why didn't you call?"

Teen: "I lost track of the time."

Parent: "What do you mean you lost track of the time? You know you're supposed to be home at six-thirty. You're getting as irresponsible as those so-called 'friends' of yours."

Notice where the focus is. It is on your teen! How do you turn that situation around and focus on you?

You begin by realizing that although you may not be able to control many aspects of your teenager's behavior, you are in control of your own actions. Therefore, instead of putting all your efforts into "convincing" your child to change, you make an impact by concentrating on what *you* can do.

Using the above situation as an example, you might begin the dialogue with, "I am serving dinner at six-thirty, and after that I am off duty." As you can see, this new statement changes the focus from "what the teen did" to "what I can do."

We have changed the focus by replacing questions and accusations that spotlight your teen's behavior with a simple direct statement that puts the spotlight on you and your action.

Translating Questions and Accusations

One way that you can begin to change the focus is by limiting your questions for one week. If you find this impossible, try one day at first. Don't give up—you can learn to replace many questions with statements about your own behavior, as we did in the example—and you may find that some questions aren't even necessary.

Let's look at the following for some additional examples.

Instead of asking these questions:

"Why didn't you fill the car with gas before returning it?"

"Why do you always leave dirty dishes in the den?"

try these statements:

"*I want* the gas tank to be filled when you use the car."

"*I expect* the dirty dishes to be put in the dishwasher."

Instead of making these accusations:

"How dare you run up a huge telephone bill with all your long-distance calls!"

"You should've told me earlier that you needed your baseball uniform washed by this afternoon."

try these statements:

"*I see* your part of the telephone bill is fifteen dollars, and *I'd like* it to be paid by the end of the week."

"*I want* twenty-four-hour notice when you expect clothes cleaned by a certain time."

or

"*I do not* have time to take care of it."

Your decision to focus on your own behavior is a significant beginning in changing the parent-teen relationship. Your sense of powerlessness and helplessness will start to lift as you take control of your own behavior, and the hostile exchanges between you and your teen will diminish.

SUMMARY

Changing Your Attitude

1. Stick with the parenting approaches that have been working for you.
2. Develop a new attitude that relieves you from feeling totally responsible for your teen's behavior.
3. Realize that your happiness does not have to be bound to your teen's behavior.
4. Change the emphasis from "what the teen did" to "what I can do."

II

Letting
Go

2

Letting Go

Kid-Life Problems

Write out a list of things that your teenager does that bother you. This list will be the basis of the work in this manual, and we hope to help you come up with a plan of action for each item on your list.

Let's say these are some of your problems:

- mistreats my personal belongings
- won't go to school
- doesn't do household chores
- lies to me

- uses drugs
- blasts stereo at all hours
- doesn't complete homework
- leaves messes everywhere
- is belligerent to me
- won't clean his room

Let's divide the problems into two lists. As you look it over, ask yourself what items *primarily* affect your kid's life and not yours. Also ask yourself which are the problems that you have little if any ability to effectively follow through with consequences. For example:

- doesn't complete homework
- won't go to school
- won't clean his room

These kinds of problems will be grouped together, and will be called Kid-Life problems.

You may feel that many of the items on the Kid-Life list do affect you in some way. Later on in the manual we will help you determine how to deal with the part of the problem that affects you directly, but for now, let's turn our attention to the teen's problems.

We suggest that you let go of trying to control your teen's behavior and turn the responsibility of these Kid-Life problems over to your child. Your immediate response to this idea may be, "There is no way I can

allow my child to decide by himself. Those kinds of decisions could affect his entire future."

This is an understandable response, particularly because parents believe it is their job to protect their child from the hardships that the teen can bring on himself. However, this kind of attitude can move parents to take full responsibility for all of their kid's decisions. **Ultimately, they can make the mistake of confusing love for their child with how much they do for their child.** They make themselves available to help in any way possible, and soon both the parent and teen end up expecting the parent to be the problem-solver.

The teen leaves the worrying to the parent while he enjoys the light-hearted feeling of being irresponsible. It's easy to fall into this habit, but by allowing this, you deprive the child of the security of knowing that he can find solutions to his own problems. You deprive him of:

1. the excitement and pride he can feel when complimented on his decisions, and
2. the lesson he can learn from his mistakes.

By helping less you allow your teen to test his own decision-making and to learn that he can count on himself and begin to take command of his own life.

When you turn responsibility over to your teen, you are showing faith in his ability. Your faith is the greatest form of encouragement for him to grow into a healthy, responsible adult.

Letting Go of Kid-Life Problems

When you start to let go of Kid-Life problems, DON'T PANIC—you don't have to let go all at once. Think of it as an experiment.

First, choose a problem, one that is clearly a Kid-Life problem and would be easy for you to let your teenager handle without your involvement. When you let go of the problem, you will also let go of scolding, disapproving, advice-giving, and other attempts to control him. It is important to begin with "minor" issues so that you can live with your child's decision. If you initially choose a critical item, you may find it very difficult not to intervene in your child's decision-making.

Some examples of Kid-Life problems that parents might turn over to their teen are the teen's choice of clothes or the way he keeps his room.

Instead of using these situations to assert your control over your teen, usually with little or no effect, you can see them as an opportunity to recognize your child's decision-making ability. For some parents, having a neat room or being properly dressed is a very important issue. If this is the case in your household, begin with a different Kid-Life problem. As we stated previously, it's essential that you choose something that is comfortable for you.

As parents let go of more significant Kid-Life problems, they may begin to feel worried or fearful of the choices their teens make. This is perfectly natural because parents want only what is best for their children. However, in wanting the best, parents sometimes forget that there are limits to what they can do. They frustrate themselves by believing that if they do the "right thing," the child will do what is "right." This

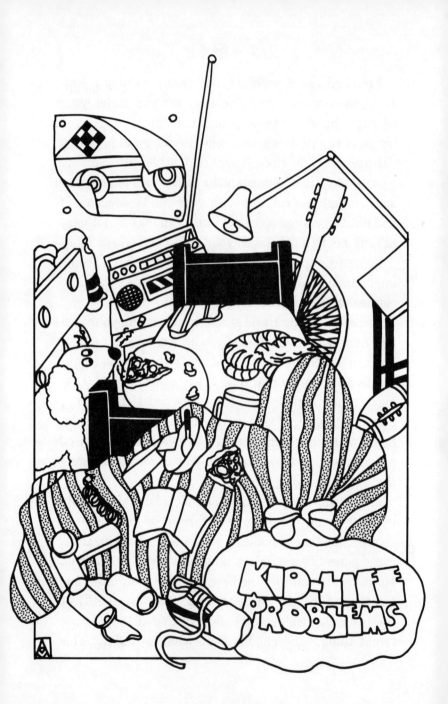

KID-LIFE PROBLEMS

can lead parents down a path of trying numerous approaches to reach the child. If each new attempt fails, parents may feel more frustrated and assert more control over the teen. What can eventually happen is that the parents find themselves in a paralyzing struggle with their teen, and little gets accomplished regarding the problem. By letting go of the Kid-Life problem, a parent can let go of the power struggle. **He can allow the teen to struggle constructively with the issue rather than struggle with the parent.**

A Kid-Life problem that many parents find difficult to let go of is supervising their children's *homework*. This is due to the fact that achieving at school seems so bound up with a child's future. Parents put themselves in the uncomfortable position of policing this activity and scrutinizing the teen's every move. They don't allow the child to experience the consequences of receiving poor grades (e.g., summer school, ineligibility for extracurricular activities).

Here's an example of what happens in many households regarding this issue:

Mr. C. did everything possible to help his child develop good study habits. In an effort to make his reluctant daughter do her homework, he tried many tactics. He sat with her each evening to make sure the assignments were completed. He insisted that she have a two-hour study period in her room without interruptions from the telephone, stereo, or television, and finally he grounded her and withdrew her privileges.

Mr. C.'s daughter thwarted him every step of the way. She "forgot" to bring home her assignments; she fell asleep on her bed during the study period, and she began lying and sneaking out of the house. Mr. C. knew he was beaten. He had started out as the taskmaster and ended up the slave to his child's decision about her homework.

He was ready to give up his job of policing and turn over the responsibility to his teen. He told her:

> "I feel worn out trying to get you to do homework. I'm exasperated because nothing I've done has worked. From now on, I'm not going to interfere with your homework. I know you're capable, and I know you'll do what's right for you."

By making this statement, Mr. C. removed himself from a power struggle that he felt he could never win. While he continued to want his daughter to do her homework, he realized that he could not force her. Therefore he changed his course of action and stopped struggling with his teen. What he did instead was state his position in a calm, clear manner without making accusations or demands.

The communication skills used in this statement were organized by Robert Bayard, Ph.D., and Jean Bayard, Ph.D., the authors of *How to Deal with Your Acting-Up Teenager*. Let's take a closer look at them.

The Three Steps to
Letting Go of the Responsibility

Communication skills	Examples
STATE your feelings and thoughts.	I feel worn out trying to get you to do homework. I'm exasperated because nothing I've done has worked.
TURN OVER the responsibility.	From now on, I'm not going to interfere with your homework.
SHOW trust.	I know you're capable, and I know you'll do what's right for you.

Notice that the statement is brief and clear, so that the teen will listen and understand. **It is important to let go of the problem in a way that reflects a loving, respectful attitude so that the teen realizes that you are giving him responsibility rather than just giving up.** In this way, letting go becomes another way that you can demonstrate your love for your child.

As we continue, we will be presenting additional

skills that you may choose to incorporate when you turn over the responsibility. In addition, we will discuss in more detail how you can take action on issues that affect you, but for now, let's focus on what may happen after you turn over the responsibility.

When Your Teenager Baits You

Let's assume you have taken the first step of turning responsibility over to your teen. Then, guess what happens? Many kids act even worse than before. Look at it this way: If you had someone take responsibility for your life, would you suddenly be willing to give that up? Of course not—at least not without a struggle.

So your teenager may try to hook you into taking back the responsibility. Remember, teenagers can be experts at dangling the bait. Before you know it, you may find yourself responding to questions such as:

"Did anything from school come in the mail?"

"Did my teacher call you?"

Step back for a moment so you can begin to realize what is going on. Now it is your teenager who is asking the questions. He is even broaching a subject that may

spell trouble for him. This is your cue that you have succeeded. He is experiencing the discomfort that can come with taking on responsibility, and he wants to dump it back into your lap.

His questions and comments are inviting you to take back his responsibilities and play the role of the bad guy. He is testing you, and this time you're ready for him. You will no longer allow your teen to cast you in the role of villain—no matter how hard he tries.

Parent: "Yes, the mail came, and you received a notice from school."

Teen: "Didn't you open it?"

Parent: "No, here it is. Also, the teacher called to tell me you missed three assignments last week."

Teen: "I really meant to get them in on time, but I just didn't have time."

Parent: "When I first found out, I was upset because I had hoped you'd buckle down at school. At this rate, you may end up in summer school or be left back and not have any education or skills to find a job."

Teen: "What are you going to do about it?"

Parent: "I don't know. I understand that you feel pressured. I would like you to do well in school, but I realize I can't make you study. However, I'd be willing to help you in some reasonable way."

Teen: "Well, I will have all of my homework done by tomorrow."

Parent: "That is up to you. I know you will do what's good for you. I do want you to know that I told your teacher today that I'm not going to sign your assignment sheets."

Teen: "You told Mr. Jones that! You can't do that—the school said that you have to check and sign my assignment sheets."

Parent: "After we talked, we agreed that my signing your assignment sheets has not been helpful. So I'm not going to sign your work anymore, and the school understands what I'm doing."

Let's review the skills used in this dialogue.

Helpful Communication Skills

Communication skills	Examples
DESCRIBE only what you see without judging.	The mail came, and you received a notice from school. Also, the teacher called to tell me you missed three assignments last week.
STATE your feelings and thoughts.	When I first found out, I was upset because I had hoped you would buckle down at school.
POINT out possible consequences.	At this rate, you may end up in summer school, or be left back and not have any education or skills to find a job.

RECOGNIZE teen's feelings.	I understand that you feel pressured.
EXPRESS what you want while acknowledging your lack of control.	I would like you to do well in school, but I realize I can't make you study.
OFFER some help.	I'd be willing to help you in some reasonable way.
SHOW trust.	I know you will do what's good for you.
ADDRESS the part of the problem that affects you directly.	After we talked, we agreed that my signing your assignment sheets has not been helpful. So I'm not going to sign your work anymore, and the school understands what I'm doing.

This last statement deals with the part of the problem that affects you. In addition, it is a place where you can effectively take action and follow through. While it is important to encourage your child to take responsibility for his behavior, it is just as important to recognize and attend to your part of the problem. Here you can begin to exert your energy and your rights in a respectful, fruitful way. Let's take a closer look at your part of the problem.

Asserting Yourself
on Your Part of the Problem

Often parents work so hard at trying to control the entire Kid-Life problem that they are not able to separate out the part of the problem that *directly* affects them. They spend all their energy trying to tell their teen what to do and are left feeling too drained to assert their own rights or take effective action to resolve the problem. By addressing the part of the problem that does affect them, parents not only take control of their own lives but also integrate respect for the child's decision with respect for their own values. To show how you can attend to your part of the problem, we will turn our attention to *truancy*—an issue that clearly affects both teen and parent.

Let's take the case of Mrs. J. The more her son missed school, the more angry and frustrated Mrs. J. became. She made numerous attempts to get her son to go to school, but none of her efforts seemed to make an impact.

Mrs. J. knew she had to do something different. Her last-ditch effort was to escort her son to and from school daily. She reorganized her days around her son's school schedule. It did not work. Her son just left school as soon as he saw the car pull away. Mrs. J. felt that she had exhausted every possible option;

she was emotionally and physically drained. She was ready for a change; Mrs. J. was ready to take the burden from her own shoulders and place it where it rightfully belonged—on her son.

Using the communication skills already mentioned, she turned over the responsibility to her child and asserted herself on the part of the problem that directly affected her life.

"I have been worried about your not going to school, and I feel frustrated about what to

do. I know you've been feeling hassled by me.
From now on, it's up to you to work out your
attendance record with the school. I want you
to know that I will not talk to school officials
without your participation."

Let's see how the communication skills we have previously discussed are applied in this example:

Communication skills	Examples
STATE your thoughts and feelings.	I have been worried about your not going to school, and I feel frustrated about what to do.
RECOGNIZE teen's feelings.	I know you've been feeling hassled by me.
TURN OVER the responsibility.	From now on, it's up to you to work out your attendance record with the school.
ADDRESS your part of the problem.	I want you to know that I will not talk to school officials without your participation.

Again, the questions and accusations that are typ-
ically spoken by parents—"Why didn't you go to

school? . . . You'll never amount to anything"—are replaced with specific, observable, nonjudgmental statements. The unheeded advice, "You should go to school," is replaced with a clear, concise statement about your own action.

Major Kid-Life Problems

There are some Kid-Life problems so serious that they require more parental involvement. These are problems where the area of control lies with the teen, but for reasons such as life-threatening consequences, legal implications, or strong parental values, the parents must pull rank and take over. When teenagers choose actions that can endanger health and lives, they are demonstrating that they have lost the ability to make responsible decisions for themselves. Consequently, parents will want to increase their role in the decision-making process.

Examples of issues that can fall into Major Kid-Life category are sexual behavior, responsible driving, and drugs. Due to the critical nature of the problem of drug use, we would recommend getting professional help if you suspect that your teen is abusing drugs. We also suggest that you begin to make some changes by turning over the responsibility to your teen and taking a stand on your part of the problem.

You can begin to turn over the responsibility to your teen by allowing him to experience the consequences of his drug-related behavior, assuming they are not life-threatening. For example, if your teen drives his car into a ditch, leave it there; if your teen becomes sick, let him clean up his mess. By leaving the evidence of his drug abuse, you make it more difficult for him or you to deny the problem. Breaking down the denial system that surrounds this illness is often the first step toward getting help.

Another way to refuse to cooperate with your teen's drug use is to take a stand where you do have control. Even though you can't stop your teen from taking drugs when he is away from home, you can take action where you are directly involved. You can insist that your home is free from drugs and paraphernalia, or you can refuse to bail your child out of the trouble his drug use creates. In this way, you make a firm commitment to do something about the problem without trying to do the impossible—monitor your teen twenty-four hours a day.

This approach may not change the teen's drug use. However, if you are going to live under the same roof with your teen in spite of his refusal to stop using drugs, you need to know that you are doing all you can.

Again, if you think your teen has a problem with

drug abuse or chemical dependency, we suggest you talk to a professional. Even if your teen is initially unwilling to go for help, a skilled professional can help your family deal with the problem and often find a way to bring the teen in for assessment.

SUMMARY

Letting Go of Kid-Life Problems

1. Turn over the responsibility.
2. Avoid your teen's baiting you into taking back the responsibility.
3. Express your views and feelings and offer encouragement.
4. Address your part of the problem.

III

Taking
a Stand

3

~~~~~~~~~

Taking a Stand

Asserting Parental Rights

We have discussed how you can let go of Kid-Life problems and allow consequences to teach your child the importance of responsible decision-making.

Now we will present ways for parents to take a stand on Parent-Life problems. This process can bring about a much improved relationship with your teen and a better feeling about yourself. We would like to suggest that you spend several weeks making the shift into standing up for yourself on Parent-Life problems because you are working toward a very basic change in the parent-teen relationship. Remember—it took your child many years of practice to become such an expert at giving excuses when you ask him to do something. Give yourself a break, and realize it will take some time to change things. Keep the faith—it will work!

Let's go back to the original list and separate out the Parent-Life problems:

- blasts stereo at all hours
- mistreats my personal belongings
- doesn't do household chores
- leaves messes everywhere
- lies to me
- is belligerent to me

You may find that some of the Parent-Life problems, particularly those that center on your teen's attitudes, such as

- lies to me
- is belligerent to me

have already diminished since you let go of Kid-Life problems. Quite simply, when parents stop playing detective by asking too many questions and stop making derogatory comments about their kids' behavior, teenagers do not have as much occasion to substantiate their case with lies and defensive maneuvers. In addition, when parents demonstrate faith in their chil-

dren's decision-making abilities, teenagers often take
this as a form of encouragement and act accordingly.

However, it is almost a sure bet that when it comes
to a major change of the teen's behavior, you probably
will have an opportunity to practice the following four
steps developed by Robert and Jean Bayard in *How
to Deal with Your Acting-Up Teenager:* negotiate an
agreement, insist with persistence, take action, and
arrange a limited strike.

The Four Steps to Taking a Stand

STEP 1
Negotiate an Agreement

You are going to begin to negotiate an agreement
with your teen around a Parent-Life issue. It is essential that you begin your work by taking one specific
example of a Parent-Life problem. First, decide which
one you want to tackle.

Here are some examples of clear-cut Parent-Life
issues:

> Your teenager blasts his stereo from the mo-
> ment he gets home until he goes to bed, your

head is in pain, and there is no relief from the noise.

Your child has to have a pair of jeans washed and dried immediately and takes your clothes out of the dryer so he can dry his. Yours are left dripping wet.

Your teenager decides he must have a snack, and then leaves every bit of evidence present to greet you when you walk into the kitchen.

You want help bringing in the groceries, and everyone seems to disappear from sight.

It is quite possible that on some issues you will be able to take care of your needs by making a clear statement of your expectations:

"When you listen to your stereo in your room, I want your door closed so I don't hear the music."

"When you take my clothes out of the dryer, put them back and make sure the dryer is turned on."

"When you fix yourself a nighttime snack, please clean up the kitchen."

Your teen may go along with you because you're taking care of yourself without limiting his needs. Your rights can coexist with those of your teen.

However, if you're still having difficulty, try the following communication skills. We will use the example of bringing in the groceries, but these skills can be used with other Parent-Life issues as well.

HOW TO NEGOTIATE AN AGREEMENT

Communication skills	*Examples*
MAKE a clear statement about what you want and your willingness to negotiate.	I want a different way of handling chores because I end up doing all the work now. I want to try to work out something together.
STATE what you think would be a fair agreement.	I think it would be fair if I shopped for the groceries and you put them away.
WORK out a negotiation with your teen, using input from *both* of you. After you reach an agreement, summarize.	When I shop I'll have them bag the perishables and nonperishables separately. I'll put away the perishables, and you'll put away the nonperishables.

STEP 2
Insist with Persistence

It is time now to test out your negotiated agreement. You may be one of the fortunate parents whose teenager says, "Sure, no problem," and then completes his chore—but don't bank on it. More than likely, your teenager will not change just because you successfully completed Step 1. Your teenager will probably want to flex his muscles and test your firmness.

In the following conversation, the teenager refuses to bring in the groceries and also successfully maneuvers you into giving her attention for negative behavior.

You have gone shopping and you say, "The groceries need to be brought inside and put away."

Teen: "Can't it wait until I'm off the phone?"

Parent: "We made a deal. It is obvious you don't remember."

Teen: "Why don't you ask sis? She never does anything."

Parent: "She just cleaned the dog messes YOU were supposed to do, but never got around to. Now get off the phone!"

Teen: "All right, all right, just give me another minute. Isn't it important I get my homework assignment? You know you always say homework comes first."

Parent: "Oh, all of a sudden you care about homework. That's a switch. You didn't seem to care last week when you didn't study for the exam you flunked."

Teen: "You just don't understand. It wasn't my fault. Most of the other kids flunked too. It was an unfair test!"

Parent: (Ten minutes later) "Get off that phone NOW!"

Teen: "I said I will in a minute!"

Parent: (Yelling) "So help me, I will disconnect the phone!"

Five minutes later the parent disconnects the phone, the teenager runs out of the house screaming that no one cares what happens to her, and the groceries are still in the car.

The child has successfully made herself look like the victim and avoided doing the chore. You feel angry, frustrated and defeated, and to make matters worse, you end up putting the groceries away. Is there no justice in the world?

In the next example, the teenager still doesn't put away the groceries, but she does not successfully bait you into giving her attention or getting you off the track.

Teen: "Can't it wait until I'm off the phone?"

Parent: "I see you're on the phone—*and* I want the groceries put away."

Teen: "Why don't you ask sis? She never does anything."

Parent: "I know you think I should ask your sister—*and* I want the groceries put away."

Teen: "All right, all right, just give me another minute. Isn't it important I get my homework assignment? You know you always say homework comes first."

Parent: "I know you are getting your homework assignment—*and*—I want the groceries put away."

You're not justifying, you're not defending your position, and you're not emphatically claiming you have a fair and caring attitude. Your statements demonstrate that you heard what she said, and at the same time you are sticking to accomplishing what you want. You stay on the task despite your teen's valiant effort to get you off track.

The skill that is used in this instance is a three-part assertive statement: "I know you would like to finish your phone conversation, *and* I want the groceries put away." Here's how it works:

THREE-PART ASSERTIVE STATEMENT

Communication skills	Examples
SUMMARIZE calmly what your teen said.	I know you would like to finish your telephone conversation
USE the word *and* instead of the word *but* to demonstrate that your teen's needs and your needs can coexist.	AND
MAKE a short statement expressing what you want.	I want the groceries put away.

Don't become discouraged. Even if the short-range goal of putting away the groceries was not achieved, you have accomplished the goal of taking care of yourself in a respectful manner. You have made this step a success if you have been persistent in a polite and relaxed manner, and if you have not become sidetracked by answering questions or scolding. Remember, you may need to try this step two or three times before you see any results.

STEP 3
Take Action

If you continue to let go of Kid-Life problems while you begin to take care of your needs, you should see some improvement in your teen's willingness to cooperate with you. If not, it's possible that your teenager still may not believe that you really will stand up for yourself. He's going to be in for some surprises when you start Step 3.

Step 3 is a move designed to establish in your teenager's mind that you can be counted on to do what you say. This step is different from the first two because it moves you from talking into taking action. So, take a deep breath and get ready for a shift to a new direction. You want to establish an entirely new notion—that you do what you say. This is called changing the balance of power, and it can be fun.

Here is how to go about it.

A. State what you want, using a calm, relaxed statement that keeps the focus on the issue.

"I want the nonperishables put away within the next hour."

"I will pay you for mowing the lawn, and I want it done by Friday."

"I don't want your coat hung up on the floor."

"I want your clean socks put away after I do the laundry."

B. When the situation arises again, say what you are going to do if the task is not completed. **Choose an action that is clearly related to the problem so that your focus is on completing the task rather than punishing your child:**

"If the nonperishables aren't put away, I'm going to leave them in the car."

"If the lawn is not mowed by Friday, I will pay the neighborhood boy to do it."

"If your coat is not hung up in the closet, I will put a cardboard box outside and toss your coat into it."

This step can be especially effective when you incorporate humorous, zany ideas into your action.

"If the socks are not put away by this evening, I will hang them on the chandelier."

C. Move into action.

Now it's time to show that you can be counted on to do what you say by moving into action. Your intent is to establish your credibility, as well as to teach your teen to help with the chores. Keep in mind that you are working toward the long-range goal of being taken at your word rather than teaching your child a lesson or taking revenge.

STEP 4
Arrange a Limited Strike

By now, we think you will have found improvements in your relationship with your teen. If, however, you have systematically followed the steps in this manual and still feel exasperated and defeated, it's time to take away what kids can take for granted and move to Step 4—limited strike. Sometimes it is very tempting to move to this action without going through the first three steps. DON'T! It assumes that negotiation will not work between you and your teen.

What we are suggesting in Step 4 is that you look over the things you do for your child, things that may be expected rather than appreciated. Find something that you can stop doing for your teen. For example, you can stop doing his laundry, cooking for one week, chauffeuring, etc.

Don't be afraid to do something that will affect other family members. Be specific and set a clear time limit so everyone will know what to expect.

Once you have decided what action you will take, tell your teen in a short statement that keeps the focus on you.

> "I'm tired of doing all the work without help
> from others. I have decided not to cook dinner
> for the rest of the week. If I don't cook, then

I don't have to worry about getting help bringing in the groceries."

"I'm not doing your laundry for the rest of the month. I am going to use the time that I usually spend washing and ironing to do the yard work because that has been neglected by you. I feel like I've been making all the compromises. Now I'm going to take care of things around the house that matter to me."

What you hope to accomplish with a limited strike is to demonstrate that you won't be taken for granted, and you will take care of yourself. More important, your teen can begin to experience the consequences when there is a lack of *mutual cooperation* in any relationship, and this is a great lesson.

SUMMARY

Taking a Stand on Parent-Life Problems

Step 1: Negotiate a fair deal with your teen that is agreeable to both of you.

Step 2: If your teen doesn't honor the negotiation, be persistent, using the three-part assertive statement.

Step 3: Establish the credibility of your word by taking action.

Step 4: Arrange a limited strike.

IV

Workbook

4

Workbook

Getting Practical

This section of the book will give you an opportunity to further develop the skills we have already discussed. In addition, we have included some guidelines that you will find helpful. We will present a series of specific exercises designed to take you in greater detail through the processes just described. The exercises are arranged in systematic progression so that you build on your skills as you proceed.

We will progress from less serious to more serious

problems, and we urge you to do the same when you put your skills into action with your family. We know that when parents are feeling desperate, they want to make major changes immediately. Please don't.

By beginning with less significant issues, you give yourself the opportunity to master the skills before tackling more difficult issues. Remember, your goal is not just to learn to deal with a specific problem or group of problems but to learn a new problem-solving method you can apply to any situation.

EXERCISE 1

Identifying Attitudes

(See pages 3–8.)

As if it's not bad enough that kids can discourage their parents, parents often end up discouraging themselves. They do this by adopting attitudes that leave them feeling helpless.

Holding on to discouraging attitudes only maintains the chaos in the household and makes it difficult to create positive change. Therefore, the place to begin in this process of change is with your own attitude.

Guidelines

1. Attitudes often take the form of internal messages that we say to ourselves.

2. Keep in mind that your new attitude should reflect your belief that your teen can be a capable, responsible person.

Examples of How to Change
Discouraging Attitudes

How I Discourage Myself	*How I Can Encourage Myself*
1. It's never going to be any different. He'll never change.	I can change my life by changing my *own* behavior.
2. It's all my fault.	He is his own person. I can give him support, and he has to learn to make decisions.

Action Step: Identify your discouraging attitudes and translate them into new sentences that you can use to encourage yourself. By saying your new sentences to yourself, you are taking the first step toward change.

EXERCISE 2

Translating Questions and Accusations

(See pages 9–11.)

In talking with their teens, parents often ask too many questions and make accusations. This tends to put teens on the defensive and often encourages lying and a belligerent attitude.

This exercise will focus on how to translate questions and accusations into statements using the phrases "I'd like," "I want," "I expect." By making these changes in your language, you not only minimize power struggles, but you will begin to set clear expectations in your household in a respectful manner. These changes in your language also increase the chance that your teen will hear what you have to say.

Guidelines

1. Minimize blame by keeping the word "you" out of your statements.
2. Don't ask questions that corner your teen.
3. Be sure to make your expectations clear—be as specific as possible. You may use time as a way to be specific, i.e., "I want the den clear of dishes by 2:00 P.M."

4. When translating your statements, be sure to choose the verb that best expresses how strongly you feel about an issue. "I wish" is less emphatic and can be used to express your values. "I expect" is more emphatic and should be used when setting rules.

Examples of Translating Accusations and Unnecessary Questions

Old Statement:	Where is my blouse you borrowed?
New Statement:	I expect my blouse to be returned in clean condition by tomorrow, or I will not lend my clothing.
Old Statement:	You only talk to me when you want something from me.
New Statement:	I would like to spend some time talking with you, or set up a time so we could do something together.
Old Statement:	Get your books out of here NOW!
New Statement:	I expect the countertop to be clear of your books in the next fifteen minutes so that I can prepare for dinner.

Old Statement: You'd better call me before you leave the house or else!

New Statement: I'd like a phone call before you leave the house so I know what your plans are.

Old Statement: Why don't you get to bed at night so you can get up in the morning?

New Statement: I wish you'd get to bed by 11:00 P.M. so you could get up in the morning.

Old Statement: Don't you dare use that kind of language with me.

New Statement: I don't talk to you that way, and I don't expect to be talked to that way.

Old Statement: You always ask for your money first, and then you never do any chores.

New Statement: I expect chores to be done before I give any more money.

Action Step: Limit your questions for a week. Write down questions and accusations that you often say to your teen. Translate them into statements.

EXERCISE 3

Make the Problem Specific

(See pages 15–16.)

One reason parents have difficulty making changes is that they don't break problems down into specific, concrete issues. Instead, they overwhelm themselves by trying to tackle a situation that is vague, and they set themselves up to be frustrated.

In this exercise we will teach you how to make problems more manageable by changing them from general/vague to specific/concrete issues.

Below is a list of typical difficulties that parents experience with their teens:

- hateful toward family members
- lies to me
- keeps emotional distance
- has to look like everyone else
- can't take responsibility for himself
- doesn't care about anyone else
- uses drugs
- uses poor judgment

What we will do is take each item on the list and translate it into a specific incident that you can address.

Guidelines

1. The problem should describe a particular behavior, not a general attitude or characteristic of your teen.

2. You know it is clear when you can visualize a picture of the problem in your mind's eye.

3. Make sure you deal with only one problem at a time.

Examples of Moving from General to Specific Problems

1. General/Vague: Hateful toward family members

   Specific/Concrete: Fights with brother and sister

2. General/Vague: Lies to me

   Specific/Concrete: Promises not to have parties when we are away but does

3. General/Vague: Keeps emotional distance

   Specific/Concrete: Stays in her room with the door closed and doesn't participate in family life

4. General/Vague: Has to look like everyone else

   Specific/Concrete: Has two earrings in an ear, a weird haircut, and holes all over his shirt

5. General/Vague: Can't take responsibility for himself

   Specific/Concrete: Doesn't get up for school

6. General/Vague: Doesn't care about anyone else

   Specific/Concrete: Monopolizes the telephone

7. General/Vague: Uses drugs

   Specific/Concrete: Found pot in house; came home drunk; smokes pot at friend's house

8. General/Vague: Uses poor judgment

   Specific/Concrete: Don't like his choice of friends

Action Step: Make a list of problems that you want to address. Make sure each item is a specific incident and remember to take only one problem at a time.

EXERCISE 4

Separating Your List

(See pages 16–18.)

One of the biggest difficulties parents have when dealing with problems is that they often begin to do some-

thing—anything—before developing a specific plan of
action. Because they don't develop a strategy specific
to the problem, parents fall into the trap of relying on
the same methods of discipline regardless of the problem. More often than not, this doesn't work. Before
deciding what to do, parents have to determine what
kind of problem they're addressing—a Kid-Life or a
Parent-Life problem.

In this exercise we will divide the problems listed
in Exercise 3 into these two major categories. This is
the first step in helping you determine the process that
is most effective in dealing with each situation.

Choose the category by looking at whose life is primarily affected by the problem, and whether you, as
a parent, can effectively implement change and follow
through with consequences.

Guidelines

1. NOTE: Those problems that primarily affect your
   teen and are of *crucial concern* to you are Major
   Kid-Life problems.
2. Most problems do affect both parent and teen.
   That's why you need to use the word *primarily*
   in dividing your list.

Divide the List

KID-LIFE PROBLEMS

- Fights with brother and sister
- Stays in her room with door closed and doesn't participate in family life
- Has two earrings in an ear, a weird haircut, and holes all over his shirt
- Can't get up for school
- Don't like his choice of friends
- Comes home drunk*
- Found smoking pot at friend's house*

PARENT-LIFE PROBLEMS

- Promises not to have parties when we're gone, but does
- Monopolizes the telephone
- Found pot in my house [Note: When things of this nature occur, they can be treated as Parent-Life problems. This is because you can more effectively implement consequences in your home.]

Action Step: Divide your list into Kid-Life and Parent-Life problems, and identify Major Kid-Life problems.

*Major Kid-Life problems

EXERCISE 5

Turn Responsibility Over to Your Teen

(See pages 18–25.)

Turning over responsibility to teens does three things. It teaches kids decision-making. It shows them that their parents have faith in their ability. It gives them a sense of pride when they succeed. It takes failure, however, for some kids to finally see their parents as a source of guidance. The challenge for you is to be brave enough to let your teens try, even if they fail.

This exercise is designed to take you through the process of turning responsibility over to your teen.

Choose a *minor* item on your Kid-Life problems list. Remember, the initial goal is not to make sweeping changes but to learn the process and give your teen responsibility for decision-making. It's important to choose something minor so you won't start interfering or nagging if your teen doesn't respond as you'd hoped.

Once the problem is selected, you create a "letting go" paragraph using the skills on page 24. The paragraph will consist of a "letting-go" statement surrounded by sentences that demonstrate your encouragement and support.

Guidelines

1. When you select a minor Kid-Life problem, ask yourself the following questions:

   Am I willing to change?

   Have I tried every other way?

   Will I continue to "let go" of the problem no matter what happens?

2. Turning responsibility over to your teen must be done in a loving, caring way. If you can't do that with the problem you've chosen, pick a different problem.
3. Keep in mind that **the success of your letting go does not depend on what your teen does.** You are being a responsible parent by giving your teen **the opportunity** to take care of himself and experience consequences.
4. Showing trust is a sign that you actually expect your teen to take control of issues in his life.

Examples of Turning Responsibility Over to Your Teen

PROBLEM 1.

Your child hibernates in her room with her door closed and doesn't participate in family activities.

SOLUTION

Your feelings and thoughts.

I miss spending time with you and wish you weren't in your room so much.

Turn the responsibility over to your teen.

However, it is your decision.

Demonstrate trust:

> I have to remind myself that you know how to take care of yourself, and you have a lot of things you like to do now that don't involve us.

The paragraph will look like this:

> I miss spending time with you and wish you weren't in your room so much. However, it is your decision. I have to remind myself that you know how to take care of yourself, and you have a lot of things to do that don't involve us.

PROBLEM 2.

Your kids are at constant war with one another. Only every once in a while do they bring out the white flag. Your job is that of chief negotiator, and, to be truthful, you know you should be fired because the fighting only gets worse instead of better.

SOLUTION

Express what you want while acknowledging your lack of control:

> I wish the two of you would stop fighting with each other, but I realize I can't stop you.

Point out possible consequences.

Sometimes I'm afraid that one of you will end up hurt.

Turn over the responsibility.

From now on I am going to stay out of your fights. It is up to you to work them out.

The paragraph will look like this:

I wish the two of you would stop fighting with each other, but I realize I can't stop you. Sometimes I'm afraid that one of you will end up hurt. From now on I am going to stay out of your fights. It is up to you to work them out.

PROBLEM 3.
You don't like your teen's choice of friends.

SOLUTION
State your thoughts and feelings.

I don't like the way you act when you're with those friends.

Turn the responsibility over to your teen.

But I realize it's not up to me to decide who your friends are. That's your decision.

Demonstrate trust:

I have to believe you'll do what's best for you.

The paragraph will look like this:

I don't like the way you act when you're with those friends. But I realize it's not up to me to decide who your friends are. That's your decision. I have to believe you'll do what's best for you.

EXERCISE 6

The Helpful Communication Skills

(See pages 25–29.)

Now that we've discussed the basics of turning over the responsibility to your teen, we can add to the skills presented in the previous exercise.

Skills are not only helpful in avoiding power struggles with teens, but they also give parents a way to state their values, interest, and concern. It's not necessary to use all of the helpful communication skills. Instead, choose a few that you think your teen could hear without turning you off.

Keep in mind that most of these problems require some action on the part of the parent. We will be discussing this in the next exercise. Wait until you've completed both Exercises 6 and 7 before you deal with your teen.

Guidelines

1. In all of these cases, if you can tell your teen to do something and he'll do it for you, by all means go this route.
2. If you find this process terribly hard to do, it's a good indication that you need to choose a different problem.
3. Don't get discouraged if your teen gets worse. Your kid is just trying harder to get you to take back your old job of telling him what to do.
4. Remember, encouragement is a key agent for change.

Examples of Incorporating the Helpful Communication Skills

PROBLEM 1.
Your teen doesn't get up in the morning for school.

SOLUTION
Understand teen's feelings:

I understand that you're tired of my nagging you.

"Letting-go" statement:

From now on, I'm not going to nag you to get up on time.

Offer help:

I will get the alarm clock fixed or buy a new clock radio.

Show trust:

I've seen you get up in the morning to go fishing, so I know you can do it.

PROBLEM 2.
Your son has two earrings in an ear, a weird haircut, and holes all over his shirt.

SOLUTION

Understand teen's feelings:

I know you like to imitate the latest look.

Your feelings and thoughts:

I have a hard time dealing with that kind of look.

"Letting-go" statement:

I have decided what you wear to school is your decision.

Action Step: Wait until you've completed Exercise 7.

EXERCISE 7

Separate Your Part of the Problem

(See pages 30–33.)

Now that you have let go of the kid's part of the problem, you will focus on identifying the parent's part of the problem and formulating an action strategy that you can implement. When you complete this exercise, your final product will be a paragraph that includes both "letting go" and "addressing your part of the problem." These two processes go hand in hand, and together they encourage independent, responsible decision-making in your teen. Therefore, it is best to wait until you can address both of these issues before presenting your statement to your teen.

In this exercise, we will continue with the examples presented in Exercise 6.

Guidelines

1. The parent's part of the problem often reflects the parent's values.

2. Ask yourself, "What action can I take?" This is your part of the problem. Make sure you are the subject of the sentence and you use an action verb. *I* will not *drive* you to school anymore.

3. Remember, this is the part of the problem that parents can take care of themselves and at the same time make an impact on the teen.

4. Keep the action focusing on problem-solving—*not* taking revenge on your teen.

5. There may be situations when you cannot figure out a solution that will affect the teen. Rather than beat a dead horse, you can decide what (if

anything) you will do about the problem and move on to a different issue.

6. Kids need limits, and your follow-through actions provide these limits.

Examples of Separating Out the Parent's Part of the Problem:

PROBLEM 1.
Your teen doesn't get up early enough for school.

SOLUTION

1. *Identify parent's part*

You are often late yourself because you give rides to your teen.

You find yourself in the middle between your teen and the school when you're asked to sign excuses for his tardiness.

2. *Your statement of action*

I will not *drive* you to school on late days like I have been doing.

I will no longer *sign* excuse notes. That's between you and your teacher.

By combining Exercises 6 and 7, your paragraph
will look like this:

I understand that you're tired of my nagging you.
From now on, I'm not going to nag you to get up
on time. I will get the alarm clock fixed or buy a
new clock radio. I've seen you get up in the morning
to go fishing, so I know you can do it. I will not
drive you to school on late days like I have been
doing. I will no longer sign excuse notes. That's
between you and your teacher.

PROBLEM 2.

Your son has two earrings in an ear, a weird haircut,
and holes all over his shirt.

SOLUTION

1. *Identify parent's part*

You pay for much of your teen's clothing.

Certain restaurants require appropriate dress, and
your family can't be admitted when your teen dresses
in his usual fashion.

2. *Your statement of action*

I'm *not going out* to dinner with you unless you change.

I'm going *to keep* $50 out of your clothing allowance and use it to pick an outfit that we can agree on for you to wear when we go out to dinner.

By combining Exercises 6 and 7, your paragraph will look like this:

I know you like to imitate the latest look. I have a hard time dealing with that kind of look, but I have decided it is your decision what you wear to school. I'm not going out to dinner with you unless you change. I'm going to keep $50 out of your clothing allowance and use it to pick an outfit that we can agree on for you to wear when we go out to dinner.

NOTE: If you feel the issue is not that important, you may decide to say something like "I don't like what you're wearing, but your company is more important."

Action Step: Identify the parent's part of the problem. Create a paragraph that you can use to turn responsibility over to your teen and address the parent's part using some of the helpful skills and a statement of action.

EXERCISE 8

Major Kid-Life Problems

(See pages 33–35.)

When the teen demonstrates an inability to make responsible decisions, parents must broaden their involvement. As we stated earlier in the book, this is an area where parents have a responsibility to intervene and take action. Consequently, in this exercise you will be paying particular attention to addressing the parent's part of the problem.

When dealing with Major Kid-Life problems, you will continue to use the same process:

"Letting-go" statements

Helpful communication skills

Address parent's part of the problem

You will note as you read our answers that it is not always necessary to use all of the skills. We've chosen the ones that are most helpful in making the point.

Guidelines

1. A good place to start is by letting your teen know the consequences of his behavior before the prob-

lem occurs. For example, if your teen begins to drive, let him know what will happen if he should ever drive under the influence of alcohol.

2. When dealing with problems involving drug/alcohol use, consult a professional. The professional can provide an assessment so you know what you're dealing with.

3. When problems involve the law, insurance, drugs, etc., you need to know the facts in order to protect yourself and to relate consequences to your teen.

4. When there is a drug problem, parents often fall into the "trap" of denial because they do not want to believe their teens use drugs.

5. Make sure you are willing to follow through with whatever "consequences" you decide to implement. Failure to do so will minimize the significance of the problem.

6. Don't try to deal with the problem while your child is under the influence of any drug.

Examples of Major Kid-Life Problems and Solutions:

PROBLEM 1.

Your teen comes home drunk from a party for the first time. One of his friends drove him home in your car.

SOLUTION

HELPFUL SKILLS

"Letting-go" statement:

You are going to have to be the one to take care of yourself. I can't do that for you. I wish I could convince you how dangerous drinking can be for you, but I can't force you to stay away from alcohol.

Your feelings and thoughts:

I feel scared knowing you attend parties where alcohol is served, and I worry about your safety on the road.

Offer help:

I am willing to pick you up or pay for a cab if you're in a position where there are no safe rides.

Address parent's part:

These are the house rules. I expect you to walk in from parties sober. I expect you to be driving home with someone who is sober.

If this is not the case, I will not allow you to take the car to parties. First of all, I don't trust anyone who's been drinking to make a rational decision about who can drive safely. In addition, my insurance doesn't cover another driver.

The paragraph will look like this:

You are going to have to take care of yourself. I can't do that for you. I wish I could convince you how dangerous drinking can be for you, but I can't force you to stay away from alcohol. I feel scared knowing you attend parties where alcohol is served, and I worry about your safety on the road. I am willing to pick you up or pay for a cab if you're in a position where there are no safe rides. These are the house rules. I expect you to walk in from parties sober. I expect you to be driving home with someone who is sober. If this is not the case, I will not allow you to take the car to parties. First of all, I don't trust anyone who's been drinking to make a rational decision about who can drive safely. In addition, my insurance doesn't cover another driver.

PROBLEM 2.

You know that your teen has been smoking pot on a regular basis.

SOLUTION

HELPFUL SKILLS

"Letting-go" statement:

I'm exhausted from playing detective twenty-four hours a day and trying to convince you to stop smoking pot.

Address parent's part:

I'm taking you in right now to talk to a counselor who can help us determine what level of treatment is necessary.

Your feelings and thoughts:

I'm doing this because I love you.

The paragraph will look like this:

I'm exhausted playing detective twenty-four hours a day and trying to convince you to stop smoking pot. I'm taking you in right now to talk to a counselor who can help us determine what level of treatment is necessary. I'm doing this because I love you.

NOTE: If you think your teen will be uncooperative, you should wait until you're in the car driving to the appointment before you say this.

Action Step: Choose one Major Kid-Life problem and create a paragraph using the skills we have discussed.

EXERCISE 9

Parent-Life Problems

(See pages 39–54.)

If you have followed the step-by-step approach presented in this book, you will probably find that teens are willing to cooperate on Parent-Life problems. This is because you've behaved in a respectful way toward them, and they have some sense of control over their own lives.

As you start to deal with Parent-Life problems, we urge you to begin by using the negotiation process whenever appropriate. Encourage your teens to come up with ideas about how a problem could be worked out as well as what the consequences will be if they don't fulfill their part of the agreement. The more input your teen has in setting up *reasonable* rules and consequences, the more chance you have that it will work.

Follow the four steps in order:

Step 1—Negotiating
Step 2—Insist with persistence
Step 3—Take action
Step 4—Partial strike

Often, parents become so discouraged and angry that they want to start with a partial strike to "shape up" their teen. You should resist this. Your goal is to work toward cooperation—not coercion.

Guidelines

1. Practice these skills by starting with minor issues and build to more significant issues. In this way you also decrease the likelihood that your teen will rebel as you start taking a stand.
2. Use negotiation as an opportunity to state what

you want and listen to what your teen wants. It is a time to show your teen that you can be flexible as long as your teen can set reasonable limits.

3. The purpose of Step 2—Insist with persistence—is to help you avoid the temptation to nag or "interrogate" your teen. Asking a lot of questions only encourages lying.

4. When you move to Step 3—Taking action—keep the focus on yourself and not what you want to "make" your teen do.

5. Note that it is not always necessary or appropriate to use all four steps.

Examples of Parent-Life Problems and Solutions:

PROBLEM 1.

Your teen monopolizes the telephone. You're not able to receive calls, let alone make them. Whenever you try to get your teen off the phone, you end up in an argument.

SOLUTION

Step 1. *Negotiation*

You and your teen have gone through the negotiation process and have come up with the following agreement:

When someone is on the telephone and another family member wants to use it, the person on the phone has ten minutes to end the conversation.

After 9:00 P.M., on school nights, the phone is reserved for adult use. Your teen agrees that, if she does not honor this, she loses use of the telephone the next evening.

You may find that you've solved the problem. However, if this does not work, move to Step 2.

Step 2. *Insist with persistence*

Let's assume your teen continues to use the phone after 9:00 P.M. on a regular basis, offering excuses like:

I forgot to get my homework assignment.

I have to get my ride to the game so you won't have to take me.

Use the three-part assertive statement:

I understand this is important, and it's after nine o'clock. It's my time.

I know you are arranging your ride, and it's nine o'clock. It's my time.

It's possible that your insistence will yield results, but if your teen ignores the rules and consequences, it's time to move to Step 3.

Step 3. *Take action*

Decide on an action step and communicate it to your teen in a concise manner.

> Because I haven't had the use of the telephone, I'm going to disconnect all the phones except the one in my room for three days.

NOTE: When you're not home you can lock your door. If you're feeling more charitable, leave the door open, knowing that your teen will probably use the phone. Remember, the action taken is not directed at revenge; rather, it is task-oriented. Your goal is to get reasonable use of the telephone.

Taking action gives your words credibility and shows that you expect to be treated fairly. This is an important message to send to your teens so they will be more likely to honor your agreements.

PROBLEM 2.

Your teen had a party when you were gone one evening. When you returned home, you found the house a disaster area with several pieces of furniture broken.

SOLUTION

Step 1. *Negotiation*

It is not appropriate to negotiate on whether the house gets cleaned—that is a given; however, you may be willing to negotiate with your teen on when the work is completed. You would probably like the work done within two or three days, but after talking with your teen, you come up with the following agreement:

> Our agreement is that all the work will be done in ten days. I understand that you will either get your friends to help, do it yourself, or hire and pay someone. I am willing to help you repair the table leg.

Step 2. *Insist with persistence*

Let's assume your teen creates numerous reasons why the task of cleaning and repairing the damage is impossible.

> My friends won't help.
> It doesn't look so bad.
> I don't have time because I have a big term paper due.

Here's where you can repeat your teen's statement and add your own sentence.

I know you have a term paper due, and the house needs to be cleaned and fixed within ten days.

Step 3. *Take action*

As you are nearing the ten-day deadline, you're painfully aware that very little has been accomplished. Now it's time to move into action. Come up with a statement saying what you will do.

> If the damage is not repaired, I will take money out of your bank account to pay for the cleaning and a handyman.

If your teen has no money, don't let that stop you— use creativity:

> If the damage is not repaired, you choose something of yours we can sell to pay for the repairs, or I will choose something.

PROBLEM 3.

Your teen frequently brings his friends into the house. Recently, you found evidence of drinking and pot smoking after the friends left. You don't believe your teen is chemically dependent: there's been no change in his behavior, he's a good student, and behaves appropriately.

SOLUTION

Step 1. *Negotiation*
In this instance, negotiation is not appropriate. Instead, state your expectation to your teen clearly and concisely.

> In our house I will not allow pot at all or alcohol use by anyone under age. Aside from the fact that it's against the law, it is against my personal values. I will be happy to continue to welcome your friends here with an agreement that there will be no pot or alcohol in our home.

Don't get hooked into defending your point. If you find yourself getting into an argument, move to Step 2.

Step 2. *Insist with persistence*
If your teen tries to throw you off track with statements like "It wasn't me" or "It was just one guy, no one else smoked or drank," you can use the three-part assertive statement.

> I hear you saying that it wasn't you, and I will not allow any pot or drinking in our house.

Step 3. *Take action*
After you stated the rule, you find evidence of mar-

ijuana where your teen's friends have been. It's time to move into action.

> The house is off-limits to your friends for one month. I will hire someone to stay in the house while I'm gone to make sure of this.

Action Step: Choose a Parent-Life problem and begin to take a stand by working through the four steps. Remember, this is your chance to begin treating yourself with respect and to encourage a cooperative family atmosphere.

Conclusion

Now that you've read through the book and completed the exercises, you should begin to feel comfortable with the skills. We hope that the concepts and skills presented in this book give you a framework that will help you organize your approach to parenting. Within this framework there can be many variations. Each parent has to tailor his approach to be consistent with his own values. Therefore, once you feel comfortable with the skills, adapt them to meet your parenting needs. For example, you may identify a Kid-Life prob-

lem that you cannot turn over to your teen entirely. In that case, negotiation might be a good solution for you and your teen. As long as you keep the fundamental concepts intact, you may experiment with the skills. Your goal is to keep that delicate balance between providing reasonable limits, recognizing your own needs, and developing responsible decision-making skills in your teen.

Keep in mind, when you use this process, you are demonstrating your love for your child in, perhaps, the most difficult way: by allowing him to experience the successes and failures in his life; by offering guidance and support when you'd rather take over and protect; and, most important, by giving him the opportunity to grow and to learn to respect and depend upon himself.